A DISCOURSE

ON THE

LIFE AND CHARACTER

OF

REV. GEO. DUFFIELD, D. D.

LATE PASTOR OF THE FIRST PRESBYTERIAN CHURCH OF DETROIT, AND FORMER PASTOR OF THE FIRST PRESBYTERIAN CHURCH OF CARLISLE, PA.,

BY

REV. CONWAY P. WING, D. D.,

OF CARLISLE.

CARLISLE, PENN'A.
PRINTED AT ELLIOTT'S BOOK AND JOB OFFICE.

1868

A DISCOURSE

ON THE

LIFE AND CHARACTER

OF

REV. GEO. DUFFIELD, D. D.

LATE PASTOR OF THE FIRST PRESBYTERIAN CHURCH OF DETROIT, AND FORMER PASTOR OF THE FIRST PRESBYTERIAN CHURCH OF CARLISLE, PA.,

BY

REV. CONWAY P. WING, D. D.,

OF CARLISLE.

PREACHED JULY 5, 1868.

CARLISLE, PENN'A.
PRINTED AT ELLIOTT'S BOOK AND JOB OFFICE.

1868

The facts mentioned in the following discourse, so far as not under the observation of the writer, are dependent upon historical notices in Sprague's "Annals of the American Pulpit," Webster's "History of the Presbyterian Church," and principally upon a manuscript correspondence between Dr. Duffield and the author.

"He was a good man." Acts XI: 24. "The end of that man is peace." Psalm XXXVII: 37. "The memory of the just is blessed." Prov. X: 7.

The man spoken of in these passages respectively is the "good man," "the perfect man," and "the just" or righteous man. The assertions regarding him are that his "end is peace" and that his "memory" "is blessed." The character is an admirable one; and the prospects held out are such as none are usually indifferent to. The united text presents the character, the death, and the memory of a good man.

The character is given with much brevity but great comprehensiveness. The phrase, "the good man" is used in the Scriptures interchangeably with a number of other expressions, devoting a high degree of moral worth; such as a just, a holy, a godly and a righteous man; a saint, a child of God and a servant of the Lord. It is always supposed to be heaven-derived and not a natural growth of the human heart. Luke tells us that his good man was "full of the Holy Ghost," and every specimen given in the Bible gained its excellence by renewing grace and a careful providential discipline. The various terms we have mentioned are each single aspects of the same man in different relations, for whoever possesses one moral virtue usually possesses all the others as fast as he is called to exercise them. And yet there is a wide distinction between them. Though the same man may be good and righteous, he is putting forth entirely different qualities when acting in these several relations. Though justice and righteousness are always beneficial they are generically distinct from goodness. The good man is much more than one who does good. Thousands are useful who "mean not so, nor do they in their hearts think of it." They are only instruments of a better and higher beneficence. None are truly good whose hearts are not benevolent, and goodness belongs to the soul and not to the hand. Divine precepts must not only control the conduct but be woven into the texture of the thoughts and affections and purposes. Human goodness must be like God's, love manifesting itself in ever varying forms of active beneficence, a light diffusing itself and irradiating all within its reach. Our Lord shows that one may be just and courteous to all, and yet rise no higher in virtue than many publicans and even heathen; and Paul, that while none will offer more than respect and esteem to the righteous man, "peradventure for a good man some would even dare to die."

The basis of such a character must be faith. Hence Luke accounts for the goodness of Barnabas by saying not only that he was "full of the Holy Ghost," but that he was full "of faith." "Of his own will" God begat us "by the word of truth." Moral precepts derived from the schools of philosophy, or even from the divine law have always been found ineffectual to renew the heart so as to form it to goodness. We mean not here to deny all excellence to the ordinary social virtues, but only that they can ever reach a Christian standard without Christian motives. Mere morality can only speak in a tone of authority and say "Thou shalt," and "Thou shalt not." The image she presents is often beautiful, but its beauty or authority can never make men benevolent—it addresses only principles which are feeble in our fallen nature. Moral preachers are proverbially cold and unsuccessful, and they have but a weak hold upon the masses of men. Passion and selfishness own no such sway. It is only when the evangelical preacher implants the love of Christ and stirs the depths of man's nature by the doctrines of Christ and the love of God through him, that he reaches down to the true springs of the soul.—Convince a man of sin, not of sinful conduct only but of a corruption which makes his whole life one great sin aud makes him essentially vile and worthless, then administer to him the gospel as a remedy for all the disorder, feebleness, and guilt of his soul, and you have stirred his whole being. Under the power of such motives he will henceforth live not for himself but for One who died for him. His eye has been fixed upon a living and glorious image of goodness, and as he gazes he grows into the same image from glory to glory. He becomes like his Master loving and good.

But it is not every regenerated or pious person that becomes distinguished for goodness. He must indeed by his renewed nature be benevolent and live not for himself, but the quality of goodness may not stand out so predominatingly as to be the distinguishing characteristic of his life. Our text speaks of Barnabas as if he were likely to be singled out for his goodness among good men. He was remarkable even among his apostolic companions for the kindness and benevolence of his character. There is room for great distinctions among those who give every evidence of piety. There are marked extremes of character among them. Some are faint and contracted in their apprehensions of Christ and of the gospel. They have caught true and transforming views of divine truth, but under its reigning power they are living rather formal and severely regulated lives, applying its principles more to the conscience than to the affections. Others are touched by generous benevolent motives, they are full of spiritual pulse and warmth, their sympathies with others' wants are keen and responsive, they are ingenious in devising and active in executing schemes of goodness, and they carry with them an atmosphere which every congenial nature feels the moment it is entered. Now what we mean is, that those who in an eminent sense are good men, are such as have derived their fundamental and controlling principles from the gospel of Christ, that they walk by faith and not by sight, and are in perpetual confidential intercourse with a living Redeemer. The life they live in the flesh, they live by the faith of the Son of God and under the impression of realities which they know principally by believing what they find in the Bible. Whenever they walk or wait or suffer, they feel surrounded by a cloud of witnesses, they are "looking unto Jesus the Author and Finisher of their faith."

And now I would turn your thoughts to the liviug exemplification of these truths in the life and ministry of our deceased brother and father, the former pastor of this church, of whose translation to another world we have just heard. We are exhorted by an apostle to be "followers of them who by faith and patience inherit the promises," and an inspired writer has given us a discourse in commemoration of those who had in earlier times "obtained a good report." Our text itself appears to sanction an attempt to perpetuate the memory of those who have been distinguished for piety in their lives. "As their good examples are an excellent sermon to the living, and the praising them when envy and flattery can have no interest to interpose, as it is the best and most vigorous sermon and incentive to great things; so to conceal what God hath wrought by them is great unthankfulness to God and to man."* In this sacred place, consecrated to the preaching of Jesus Christ and Him crucified, you are aware that I am in the habit of holding up any man for special distinction very sparingly and with great hesitation. The force of such examples is often broken by a knowledge of great imperfections. And I am not unmindful of all this in the present instance. But are we never to be edified by discoveries of God's grace until we can find human perfection, or until time has diminished our sense of what is defective? Is it not better to observe living models though imperfect, and conform to them even as they are conformed to Christ?

With respect to Dr. Duffield, I may remark that,

1. *He was favored by a kind Providence with many natural advantages.*

Without these it is often impossible to rise to eminence. A degenerate plant can seldom be recovered or made fruitful. *Among these advantages is a pious and godly ancestry.* In this country many persons are in the habit of depreciating the benefits of a high birth and a good family. It is thought that every man must make his own way irrespective of his family relations. But while we may concede that none deserve esteem merely because of their social position and ancestral reputation, it is vain to deny that these afford advantages which are sometimes almost indispensable and are always helpful

*Bp. Jer. Taylor's Sermons; Serm. VII, Vol. II, p. 72.

to our advancement. God never enters into a covenant with a race without using the advantages of the family relation. He made it an inestimable benefit to be connected with such families as Noah's and Abraham's and Levi's and David's and Rechab's, and he incorporated the principle in his fundimental law, that the iniquity of the fathers should be visited upon the children unto the third and fourth generation of them that hate Him, and that mercy should be shown unto thousands of generations of them that love Him and keep His commandments. The family to which our brother belonged, appears to have combined within itself contributions from the three important races, the French Huguenot, the Scotch Covenanter and the Dutch Lollard. On our first acquaintance with it, it was probably a family of refugees in the north of Ireland, from France. Its French name (DuFielde or DuVille) was there brought to its present more Anglicised form as they mingled with those Scotch inhabitants who had recently emigrated there and had become involved in conflicts with prelatical power. The great-grandfather of our deceased brother came to this country in connection with that great wave of immigration which flowed into the south-eastern counties of Pennsylvania near 1730. He purchased a farm in Strasburg, Lancaster county, which remained for several generations in the possession of the family, and even now is said to be owned by his descendants on a daughter's side. His third son, George, (a name borne by some one of each generation) was for thirteen years the pastor of the first Presbyterian congregation which was formed in our town. In 1772 he was called to the first pastoral charge of the Third or Pine Street church of Philadelphia, where he became so notorious for his zeal in behalf of Colonial liberties that a price was set by royal authority upon his head, and he was chosen by the Continental Congress as one of its chaplains. When his own congregation was temporaily broken up by the confusion incident to the war, he accompanied the revolutionary army, and did much by his patriotic discourses to animate the hearts of the soldiers during the dark days of their struggle. He was associated with that earnest and intelligent band of ministers who labored so successfully in the great revivals of religion which prevailed near the commencement of his ministry in this region, and his manuscript sermons indicate that he must have been a peculiarly awakening and discriminating preacher. His oldest son George spent most of his life on the ancestral farm in Lancaster county, though he appears to have been a merchant, and to have been the Register and Comptroller General of this State during the adminisration of Gov. Thomas McKean. He is said also to have been an active and consistent member of the Presbyterian church. He was married to Faithful Slaymaker of the same county; their son, the subject of our present notice, and their son's son, have been eminent preachers of the gospel; and all their living descendants as far as known to us, are distinguished for their zeal in behalf of our common faith. It was no small privilege to be connected with a family so manifestly within the bonds of the covenant of grace, and to be an heir to the promises: "A good man leaveth an inheritance for his children's children;" and "The children of thy servants shall continue and their seed shall be established before thee."

It is not unworthy of notice also that he was blessed with *a remarkably vigorous and healthy bodily constitution.* When we observe how many around us are rendered incapable of exertion, and how inherited disease and depravity weigh down the spiritual powers of multitudes, and subject them to brooding melancholy, or pervert them to sensuality and self-indulgence, we must see reasons for valuing highly an organization like his, favorable to buoyancy of spirits, capable of prolonged and severe toil, and never exhausted during a long life.

Nor were *his mental faculties* of an ordinary character. He had that rather rare combination of an acute logical power, a warm and glowing heart, and a will that could never be shaken from its purpose. It was a delight to him to work hard at the abstrusest theological investigations, and it was not simply from a rigid rule but from real predilection that he kept up the daily habit as far as it was practicable, of reading a portion of the Scriptures in three or more languages, often diverted himself with problems in the highest mathematics, and took part in the public discussions of societies devoted to Natural Science. Whatever one might think of his arguments he was generally able to present them with clearness and with an abundance of pertinent illustrations, and no one ever knew him to give up a conviction from a fear of consequences or from the opposition of men.

2. *His early education also appears to have been thorough.*

The worldly possessions of the family, if not large, were at least sufficient to afford him all the advantages of our best institutions without interruption or restriction. At the early age of sixteen (in 1811) he graduated at the University of Pennsylvania then under the provostship of Dr. John McDowall, who attributed his own conversion in very early life to a discourse by his pupil's grandfather at Monahan, now Dillsburg. The same year in which he graduated he entered the Theological Seminary of the Associate Reformed Presbyterian church, then under the care of Dr. John Mason, whose friendship he afterwards so abundantly enjoyed, and whose doctrinal instructions he always delighted to honor. He appears however not to have been a communicant or to have possessed satisfactory evidence of his own piety until some time after this commencement of his Theological studies, when he united with the congregation under the spiritual ministrations of the Rev. Dr. John B. Romeyn. He evidently now entered upon the service of his Master and especially upon the ministry, with a sincere love to the souls of men. He was licensed to preach the gospel by the Presbytery of Philadelphia in April, 1815, when he was three months short of twenty-one years of age.

3. *The circumstances under which he entered upon his pastoral work were especially and severely trying, but calculated to draw forth all his energies.*

It was on a journey, undertaken for his father's business as a merchant, in the month of July 1815, into the more western part of this State, that he stopped to spend a Sabbath in our borough. As the pulpit of this church was then vacant, he was invited to preach in it. For two years and eight months since the death of Dr. Davidson in December 1812, the congregation had been distracted in its attempts to obtain a successor. Old contrvoersies, which had slumbered during his long pastorate had recently reawakened, and factions had been formed whose appeals were carried up to the highest judicatories of our general church. During this time the Sacrament of the Lord's Supper had been but once administered in the congregation, the records of the church had become defective and confused, and vital piety had fallen to a very low standard. We have seen individuals who well remember the first sermon which the youthful preacher gave on his introduction to his future charge, and a number of persons ascribed their permanent religious impressions to his fidelity and zeal on that occasion.—He himself, long afterwards remembered that his soul was drawn forth on that day with peculiar earnestness and power. By the middle of the following December a call was put into his hands to become the pastor of this church, and on the last Sabbath of the year he commenced preaching here. The various parties had agreed to lay aside their difficulties and to unite in the call, though a few individuals ventured to lodge in his ears some tales of strife respecting other members of the church and of the Presbytry. These he was endowed with discretion enough to bury in silence, and the authors not long after found better themes of conversation. It was however with extreme solicitude for the result, that he ventured in February of the next year and after six weeks of labor among the people, to accept the call; and he was not even then ordained and installed until the commencement (Sept. 25th 1816) of the following autumn. He was aware that his views on some points of Theology and on the proper administration of the Sacraments were not in accordance with those of some of his people and his brethern in the ministry, and he had reason to anticipate a severe struggle on this account; but as he believed that providence was leading him he resolved to make the effort. The new regulations which his principles required, he introduced with caution and after careful private discussions with his principal friends. In a series of discourses he publicly vindicated and explained the distinction between those who belonged to Christ and those who belonged to the world, and he showed that none but the former could properly receive the Sacraments for themselve or their children. He then took his stand firmly against all those amusements which were disreputable to piety, refused to admit to communion those who persevered in them, and declined to administer baptism to the children and servants of those who could not present them in credible faith. The excitement was for some time intense, and a number of persons left the congregation and united with another in which a different practice prevailed. God however vindicated his own truth and the whole conflict was overruled to deepen very perceptibly the piety of his people. He was cordially sustained by the Session of his church, which at that time consisted of William Douglass, (who had been a member and probably an Elder in his grandfather's church) James Lamberton and George Davidson. To these were added before his first communion in October, Thomas Carothers, Thomas Urie, Robert Clark, John Irvine and Robert McCord, men of unquestioned piety, of invincible firmness and of wise counsel; and of whom he always spoke with affectionate gratitude and sincere respect.

4. The congregation thus diminished and bound to great strictness of deportment *now entered upon a career*

of prosperity. The first communion season (October 20, 1816) was an occasion of extraordinary interest. Twenty-three persons by profession and twenty-one by certificate were added to the communion. During the first year of his pastorate this number was augmented to seventy by profession and fifty by certificate. During the eighteen and a-half years in which he sustained the pastoral office here six hundred and ninety-seven persons were admitted on profession and two hundred by certificate, making an average of a little more than forty-eight persons each year. The number of people connected with the congregation was then large, since the largest portion of the population in both town and country was at that time Presbyterian, and the habit of attendance upon public worship was almost universal. There were indeed years when the heart of the zealous pastor was discouraged, and he was disposed to think he was laboring in vain and spending his strength for nought; but a healthy state of public feeling generally prevailed, the dews of divine grace uniformly descended, and some seasons were enjoyed which deserved the name of general revivals. Such were, the latter part of the year 1822 during which a hundred and nine, the beginning of the year 1827 when above thirty, the early part of 1831 when eighty-four, and the year 1834, (the last year of his ministry in this town) when seventy-eight, first professed their faith in Christ. These revivals were in every instance apparently the result of divine influences in connection with the ordinary means of grace. Sometimes when the state of public interest plainly demanded it the number of meetings during the week would be increased, and sometimes the assistance of a neighboring pastor was called in. The individual who more frequently than any other came to his aid was the Rev. Dr. Dewitt, who had made a profession of religion in the same congregation in New York city, had studied Theology under the same instructor (though at a period later by two or three years), had been settled over a neighboring congregation only two years after his own installation, though differing from him in some of his theological views had stood by him and substantially agreed with him in all his practical measures, and finally preceded him to another world by only seven months. His efforts in behalf of Temperance, in the establishment of prayer and missionary meetings, in the introduction of hymns into public worship, and in opposition to fashionable amusements need not now be particularized, but can hardly be appreciated at a time when his practice in these respects has become so successfully established. This congregation especially owes him a debt of gratitude which it has never been inclined to withhold, but we doubt not he is now receiving a richer reward in a world where nothing but grace is the everlasting song. If all who were hopefully converted under his labors were assembled together in our house of worship it would scarcely afford them room; but to these must be added a multitude who owed their impressions of truth to his faithful preaching and conversation. Many of these may finally fail of everlasting life, but they will confess that their impenitence was inexcusable under his clear exhibitions of doctrine and his affecting expostulations in and out of season.

5. Nor can I omit to mention that *he was prominent in those ecclesiastical controversies which led to the division of*

our church in 1837. I have no wish to revive the memory of those sad contentions. Few who mingled in them can recall all that was then said and done by them with unmingled pleasure. We have lived to see a time when we can contemplate those conflicts with an impartial and enlarged judgment. It is likely that each party was used by providence to modify the extreme tendencies of the other, and that both were needed to work out the result demanded by the times. Both were doubtless actuated in the main by a sincere zeal for what they looked upon as important principles. In the Dedication and Preface to a work on " Spiritual Life or Regeneration," published in 1832, Dr. Duffield remarked that " in the early period of his theological studies and for several years after the commencement of his ministerial life, he had felt extreme perplexity on that subject and had been wont to define and illustrate Regeneration according to philosophical views which he was now persuaded were incorrect. He regretted deeply the influence which these views had had upon the people of his charge, and he knew of no more suitable atonement for his fault than to give them in a volume the result of his more mature investigations." He was under an impression that many persons were in the habit of excusing themselves for their impenitence by false pleas of inability, and of sheltering themselves for their refusal to obey the gospel call under the shield of orthodox technicalities. He often heard them allege that they could not be blameable for an unbelief which resulted from a complete want of power in any sense to appreciate and accept the gospel, and that they should not be urged to seek a share in an atonement which was intended not for them but for the elect alone. Whatever grounds they had for these allegations he thought he had found doctrinal statements which were liable to no such objections, and these he honestly urged upon the hearts and consciences of his hearers. Many of them felt the power of his statements and appear to have been satisfied with them. Others thought that in his zeal for the conversion of souls, he had sacrificed important principles of truth ; and they feared that he had fallen into fundamental error. He was one of a number of ministers who were tried for heresy before the judicatories of the church, none of whom were directly condemned, but they were afterwards connected with a large party in forming a separate Branch of the Presbyterian church. The result has doubtless been somewhat different from that which either party then anticipated, but probably better for the interests of the general church than that which either would have devised. Our Presbyterian Zion, we may believe, is stronger and purer to-day than it would have been if either party had more completely triumphed. We hope the day is near when the parts then rent asunder will be reunited, and that the united body will be without some spots and wrinkles which either party would have left upon her.

6. In the midst of these contentions, but immediately after a powerful revival of religion *he became satisfied that a change of his field of labor was desirable.*

In this many thought him decidedly in an error, but the thing was doubtless of the Lord and the change was effected in March 1835. Two settlements, one in Philadelphia and another in New York, proved transient and without important results. In three years and six months after his pastoral relation to this church was dissolved, he was called to his last and longest charge in the city of Detroit. At once he accepted the call and commenced his labors there on the first day of October, 1838. Into every part of the new State which then received the benefit of his ripened zeal and experience he extended his influence, and there are few churches of our order in that region which have not come under obligations to him. It was during the latter part of the same year in which he was settled in Detroit, that I was myself settled for a short time near him, when he preached my installation sermon, and during a brief season of affliction when I was laid aside from pastoral labors he showed me the sympathy of a brother.

7. *For nearly thirty years he was there permitted to exercise his talents in the service of his Master.* Most of this time was spent in the humble labors of a faithful pastor, in which however he was eminently successful. More than once his services were called for by the general church, and in 1862 when the General Assembly met in Cincinnati, he was elected to preside over its deliberations. He found also considerable time for investigations of a learned and scientific nature, the results of which he gave to the world in a series of volumes and pamphlets, and articles in our Theological Quarterlies. These were principally on Prophesy, on Capital Punishments, on American Slavery, on the Scriptural use of Wine, on Prelatical Episcopacy, on the Distinctive Views of the Two Principal Branches of the Presbyterian Church, on the Cherubim of the Old Testament, on Secession its Cause and Cure, and other questions of the day. In all these, if he could not always carry with him the convic-

tions of his readers, he uniformly left an impression of his sincerity and candor; and he brought to each topic such an array of learning and argument which seldom left anything to be added on the side he advocated.

In 1848 he was twice violently attacked, with an interval between the attacks of only two months, by the Asiatic cholera, from the effects of which he did not soon recover. For six months he was unable to occupy his pulpit, and at the end of four years so much was his general health impaired that he was advised by his physicians to try the effects of foreign travel. Accordingly he sailed from New York in July, 1852, and spent more than a year in travelling through England, France, Italy, Egypt, the Peninsula of Sinai, and the Holy Land. His observations during this journey, in which his health was completely restored, were given to the public during his absence weekly in the New York Evangelist, and afterwards in an interesting volume. While he was absent from them his people came to the determination to erect for themselves three houses of public worship, and when these should be completed to organize themselves into three distinct congregations. In the course of two years this plan was executed with entire unanimity and success, and each new organization became as efficient as the original one had been. Last autumn (Sept. 11th), his collected family and congregation united with him in celebrating the fiftieth anniversary of his marriage with Isabella Graham Bethune, the grand-daughter of the celebrated Isabella Graham and a sister of the late Rev. Dr. Bethune. This people will also recollect his attendance (July 1st, 1857), upon the centennial celebration of the original erection of the building in which we are assembled, when he gave us the interesting historical discourse published on that occasion. As he then stood before us he remarked that he was within three days of what has been styled "the grand climacteric of mortal existence" (sixty-three years of age), and that he was "endeavoring to lift his thoughts and aspirations above the ever fluctuating events of this perishing world, so as to look more ardently to that blessed hope, the glorious appearing of the great God and our Savior Jesus Christ. Since that period his life has been protracted more than ten years, and recently he has been permitted to revisit us and to give us a parting word of warning and encouragement. On this latter occasion none listened to him without emotion, as he attempted, with a trembling voice but with a heart as warm and a pathos as tender as ever, to describe and make more attractive the christian's hope, that "when the earthly house of this tabernacle shall be dissolved he has a building of God, a house not made with hands, eternal, in the heavens;" and when he entreated, yes, *entreated as a father*, those who knew not this hope or who had relaxed their hold upon it, to give themselves no rest until they had a firm possession of it. Does it not seem as if one had been sent unto us, not indeed from the dead, but irradiated in anticipation with an opening cloud of glory to startle us that we might not so wearily loiter in our heavenward course? Scarcely had he returned to his home from this journey of love, than his increased feebleness was noticed by his friends, and it became evident that God was gathering up the little threads of his life. He moved about still among his people, visiting the sick and comforting some who had been recently afflicted; and finally was stricken down, not worn out and burdensome to himself or others, not in imbecility or attenuated by painful disease, but in the midst of his usual duties, with his armor on, and in the very place where, had he been permitted to choose, he would have asked to lie down to rest—in the pulpit and beckoning on an association of young men to their work for Christ. It was a true *enthanasia,* an easy and a happy death, such as thousands intensely pray for. He was allowed just time enough afterwards, to send for his sons, and to cast his mantle upon one of them who was emulating him in the sacred calling. Who will not regard this as a beautiful close for such a life? Surely the end of that man was peace?

And now the *memory* of such a man is blessed. It is blessed, not because trumpeted by the world's noisy acclamations. Such fame is the lot of but few among God's earnest servants, and could never satisfy their hearts. It is the proper goal for worldly ambition but not for such as desire the love of their fellow men. The world sometimes admires but seldom *blesses* those whom it celebrates. Its monuments are cold even when most splendid. But there is a sphere, and that no very contracted one in which the name of our brother shall be held in everlasting remembrance, and shall be spoken with most affectionate benedictions.

He will be recollected by many who owe to him under God the highest valuable benefits which one human being can receive from another. What a rain of blessings is often showered upon a congregation by the ministrations of such a man. How many who come each Sabbath day from their homes sad and enfeebled by life's weary trials, hear from his lips words of clear counsel, of encouragement and strength which are more valuable than gold? How many can remember the dark hour, when their souls were struggling with the terrible questions relating to eternal life and death, the wrath or the favor of the infinite Judge, and when their characters and destinies were taking shape for an everlasting existence, and when that then some faithful servant of God came forward and with a few simple words resolved their perplexities, directed them to the Rock of ages, and imparted to them a peace which passed all understanding! For his fidelity in such a work the memory of our brother is blessed.

It is blessed too because his heart was in thorough sympathy with men. The good which many do is rather from an overruling providence and because their own pleasure happens to lie in the direction of what is useful. Many find their highest virtue in pursuing their ends on account of the intrinsic desirableness of the objects themselves, rather than for the benefits they secure. Such is not the spirit of the true servant of Christ, and especially of our departed brother. The great end for which he lived was to save and bless his fellow-men. He took delight in science, in social life, and in a beautiful world around him. But he would have renounced them at any moment had they not been subservient to a higher and philanthropic aim. Others give up even life on fields of glory, but it is the enthusiasm of the conflict, and the eclat of public applause which predominate over all higher influences and give power to motives which otherwise had been feeble. But he and such as he are sustained by no such outward motives, they are impelled to action and self-denial by a simple love of man. They "honor all men" by aiming at their elevation through the only means which recognize the true nobility and totality of their being. And it is to such alone—to such as *mean* our good, who pray for it and devote their lives to it—that we can feel real gratitude, andupon their memories we bestow our sincerest blessing.

The memory of the just is blessed because their example is a great encouragement to all who follow them. Even those who have set out with the greatest resolution on the heavenward career are sometimes extremely despondent. The glorious realities of faith are lost sight of, and we are perplexed by the intricacies and delays of providence. We not unfrequently see the wicked for a long time prosperous, and the righteous cast down and apparently forsaken by providence. We hear the great world loudly calling the proud happy, and vauntingly setting on high them that work wickedness. We are startled sometimes to find that "our feet are almost gone and our steps have well nigh slipped." Then it is that when we see brethren before us, frail and trembling men like ourselves, finally reaching the goal not like shattered and shipwrecked mariners, but like gallant ships entering the quiet haven with swelling sails and a full cargo, we thank God, and take courage.

Their memory too is blessed because it assures us that the way of goodness is after all the way of true honor. When we beheld this aged Christian and minister of God after a life of continual struggle, standing before a whole community and receiving the honors and congratulations of a large circle of admirers, we could not but see that it was the homage which the world was compelled to pay to virtue and true goodness. We turn to the boasting crowds who long since refused his calls and followed crooked paths, and as we see most of them wounded or slain, we exclaim "Their rock is not as our rock, our enemies themselves being judges." Life is full of confirmations of the wise man's proverb that "the way of transgressors is hard," and that "it surely shall be well with the righteous." We "have been young" and some of us "are now old, yet have we never seen the righteous forsaken nor his seed begging bread."

Let us improve the memory of our departed brother to strengthen our faith, and to induce us to consecrate ourselves more heartily to the kind of life he commended by precept and example. All must now be satisfied even if they ever doubted it, that the words he so often spoke with pathetic earnestness were not the artificial utterances of official or interested zeal. Those who are accustomed with some shadow of suspicion to hear ministers pour forth words of intense fervor and deep solemnity may learn that such can also be faithful even unto death, and will be prepared in like manner to commend their messages in the honesty of a dying hour. Let such be persuaded to hear us with confidence whenever we speak as of the oraeles of God. Let us all go forth to our remaining work on earth, resolved to be holier, firmer to our principles, and more devoted to the only course which can end in a glorious victory. In the language of one of the last hymns our departed brother sang on earth, let us exclaim,

"What sinners value I resign,
Lord 'tis enough that Thou art mine."

www.ingramcontent.com/pod-product-compliance
Lightning Source LLC
LaVergne TN
LVHW011140110826
845150LV00008B/2425

* 9 7 8 1 4 1 8 1 9 2 8 6 0 *